Plate Tectonics and Continental Drift

Plate Tectonics and Continental Drift

John Edwards

Evans

Published by Evans Brothers Limited
2A Portman Mansions
Chiltern Street
London W1U 6NR

© Evans Brothers Limited 2005

First published 2005

British Library Cataloguing in Publication Data
Edwards, John
Plate tectonics and continental drift - (Looking at landscapes)
1. Plate tectonics - Juvenile literature
2. Continental drift - Juvenile literature
I. Title
551.1'36

ISBN 023752743X

Consultant: Simon Ross
Editor: Sonya Newland
Designer: Big Blu Ltd
Picture researcher: Julia Bird

Contents

Introduction

It is amazing to think of, but scientists believe that once, millions of years ago, all the land on Earth was joined together in one large land mass surrounded by a single massive ocean. Eventually this land mass broke apart, the pieces started to move away from one another, and oceans grew in between them. They eventually formed the continents that we know today. This movement is still happening – the continents are drifting, sometimes breaking apart, sometimes shifting closer together. They are moving very slowly, between 1 and 10 cm per year.

The reason for the movement of the continents lies deep beneath the oceans. The whole surface of the Earth is actually made up of a number of huge slabs called tectonic plates, which are in constant motion. They may move very slowly, but their sheer size means that if these plates bump into, pull away from, or grind past one another, the effects can be dramatic. Lots of strange but impressive features are formed as a result of plate movement: strings of volcanic islands in the middle of the ocean; chains of underwater mountain ranges; great trenches in the ocean floor – the very deepest and darkest places on our planet.

▶ The movement of the Earth's plates can cause volcanic islands to form. This one lies off the coast of Iceland. The craters appear when hot gases bubble up through the lava when the island is being formed.

Plate movement itself is caused by activity deep inside the Earth. The Earth's solid inner core is radioactive, and generates forces that move the softer rock in the layers above it. Temperature and pressure here are very high so the molten rock just beneath the Earth's surface 'flows', causing the plates on top of it to inch slowly but constantly in different directions.

Many of the effects of tectonic movement do not directly affect us – the processes happen so slowly that they are almost imperceptible. However, two of the most familiar consequences of plate movement can have serious effects on human life: earthquakes and volcanic eruptions. These have been occurring for millions of years and still happen frequently. Most earthquakes are so small that they go largely unnoticed, but some can be huge, and when they occur in populated areas, they can cause devastation to property and loss of life. Volcanoes are also created by tectonic movement and can be equally devastating. Although there are thousands of volcanoes all over the world, and most of them are extinct or dormant, more than 1,000 are active. When they erupt they can spew out rivers of boiling molten lava and clouds of hot dust, ash and rock. These can travel for many kilometres, destroying the surrounding land, and covering whole cities with layers of suffocating ash.

Despite these dangers, the movement of the Earth's plates has created some of the most beautiful and dramatic landscapes on Earth – and will continue to do so for many millions of years to come. In the far distant future, the features of the Earth and the position of the continents and oceans that are so familiar to us now, will be very different indeed.

▲ This fissure in the floor of the ocean – at a depth of around 2,600 metres – was caused by tectonic plates pulling apart from each other. As the plates spread, the Earth's crust is stretched and cracks form.

The Structure of the Earth

The Earth is probably about 5,000 million (five billion) years old. In the beginning, it would have been a boiling mass of molten rock and gas. It may be hard to believe, but so much heat was given off that, millions of years later, the temperature at the centre of the Earth is around 6,200°C. Our planet is still cooling down.

As the Earth began to cool, different materials started to separate out. More dense materials such as iron started to form the core of the Earth. Lighter materials such as silicates floated to the surface. Distinct layers began to form in the Earth.

The Earth as we know it today is made up of these layers. The surface or outer layer is called the crust. The crust is very thin compared with the size of the Earth – on average only 20 km in depth. If the Earth was the size of a football, then the crust would be less than 1 mm thick. The thickest and oldest crust is the continental crust, the outer layer of the Earth, which is, on average, 35 km deep. Continental crust is dominated by crystalline rocks, rich in quartz and feldspar. Some of these rocks are as much as 3.5 billion years old. Oceanic crust is much thinner and younger – only 6 km

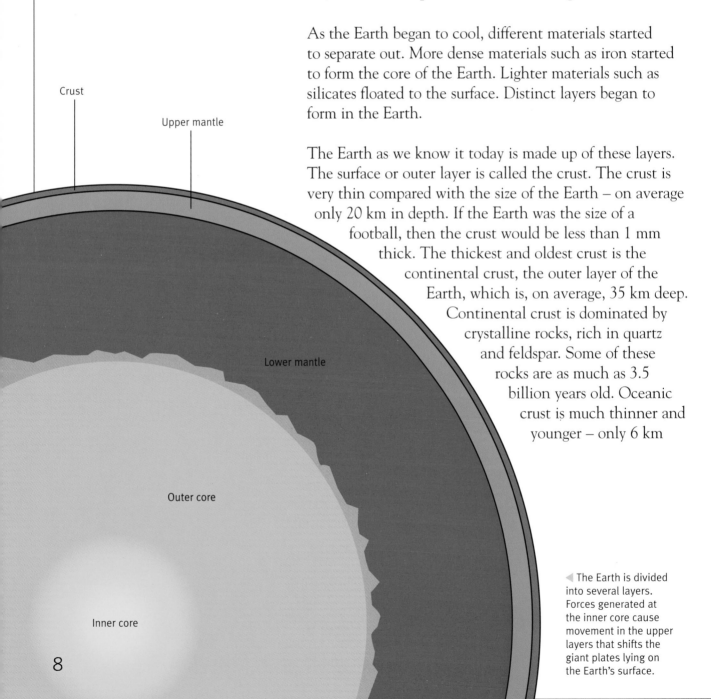

Crust

Upper mantle

Lower mantle

Outer core

Inner core

◀ The Earth is divided into several layers. Forces generated at the inner core cause movement in the upper layers that shifts the giant plates lying on the Earth's surface.

8

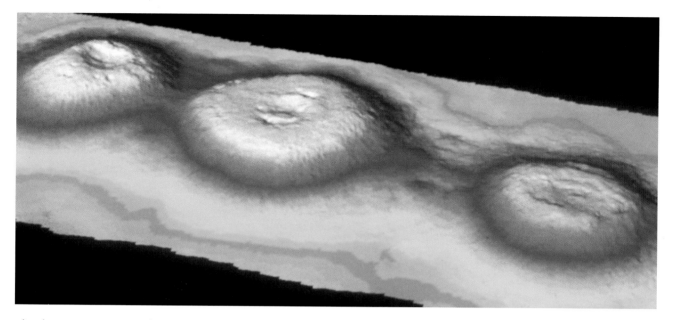

thick on average and not more than 200 million years old. Oceanic crust is largely made up of a dense rock called basalt, formed by a network of underwater volcanoes. New crust is being formed all the time.

The broken Earth

The zone of rock below the crust is called the mantle. This is nearly 3,000 km thick, and is made mostly of iron and magnesium. The mantle is divided into several layers. The upper part of the mantle is solid rock, but at greater depths it becomes molten. Rocks in the mantle are continually on the move. This movement is the root cause of the world's earthquakes and volcanoes.

The layer beneath the mantle is the core. Much of the core is iron and nickel, which is liquid because it is so hot. This liquid part of the Earth's core is called the outer core. The very centre of the Earth is the inner core. Although the inner core is also made of iron and nickel and is extremely hot, it is solid because the rocks are under so much pressure that they are pressed together.

The Earth's crust is divided into sections called plates. The Earth can be pictured rather like a hard-boiled egg. The yolk represents the core, the white the mantle, and the shell the crust. If the egg is knocked on a hard surface, the shell cracks, but all the pieces stay in position. The Earth's plates fit together like a jigsaw.

▲ A chain of underwater volcanoes – known as the Three Wise Men – situated in the South Pacific Ocean. These are part of a string of volcanoes over 40,000 km long, stretching around the world, which is constantly creating new oceanic crust.

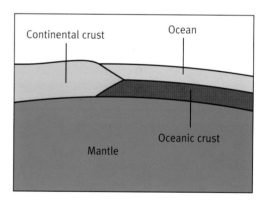

▲ Both continental and oceanic crust lie just above the Earth's mantle. Oceanic crust is covered by the seas. Continental crust rises above the ocean.

🌑 The lithosphere

The rigid shell of the Earth is called the lithosphere, from the Greek word *lithos*, meaning 'stone'. Instead of being smooth, it is broken into massive fragments. These fragments are called tectonic plates, or sometimes lithospheric plates.

The Theory of Plate Tectonics

The crust is the Earth's outer rocky shell. It is not continuous over the entire surface of the planet, but is actually broken into huge areas called tectonic plates, which lie on top of the Earth's mantle.

The plates are made up of solid rock, and they range from 6.5 km to 65 km thick. Tectonic plates vary in shape and size – there are nine large plates, as well as several smaller ones. Tectonic plates are not defined by continents or oceans; they can cut through them, as the map below shows. However, six of the nine large plates are named after the continents that lie within them: North American,

▼ Some of the plates that make up the surface of our planet are moving apart, while others are colliding. This map shows the various plates and the directions of their movement.

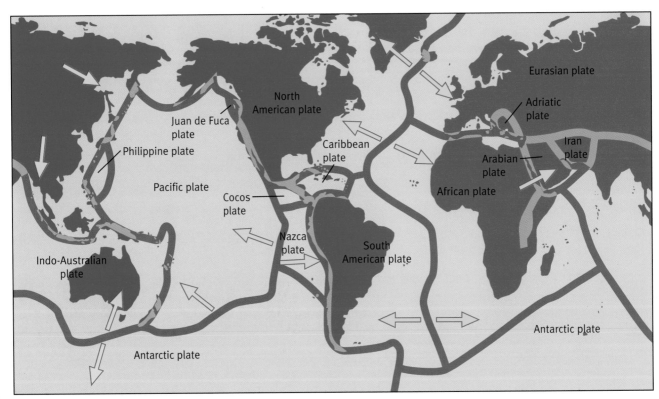

South American, Eurasian, African, Indo-Australian and Antarctic. The Pacific, Nazca and Cocos plates are oceanic – that is, there are no continents, just ocean, above them. The other plates shown might be much smaller, but their movement can have the same effects as the large plates, and they are capable of causing just as much damage on the Earth's surface.

How do we know about plate movement?

Tectonic plates are constantly moving. The North American and African plates, for example, are moving apart, while the Eurasian and African plates are colliding. The average rate of movement is between 1 and 10 cm per year. The Earth's plates are moving about the speed at which your fingernails grow! Plate movement is so slow that we cannot feel it happening, so what first gave people the idea that the Earth was made up of gigantic plates? And how did they find out how they moved around?

During the nineteenth century, scientists began to look at the shape of all the different land masses on Earth. They noticed that the east coast of South America seemed to fit together with the west coast of Africa rather like pieces of a jigsaw. The German scientist Alfred Wegener (1880–1930) suggested that perhaps they had once been joined together. If this was the case, then it was likely that all the continents had once formed a single large land mass. Over time this land mass broke up and the continents floated on the ocean floor to the positions they are in today.

▲ This image of the Earth from space shows the phenomenon that scientists in the nineteenth century began to wonder about – the shape of the east coast of South America (centre left) seems to fit with the shape of the west coast of Africa (upper right) like pieces in a jigsaw.

◄ Alfred Wegener, the German scientist who first proposed the theory of continental drift. Although evidence seemed to prove his theory, Wegener was unable to explain exactly how such massive pieces of land had broken apart and moved around, and for many years his ideas were not taken seriously.

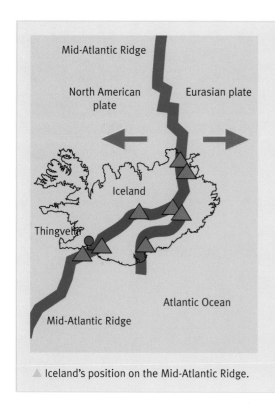

Iceland's position on the Mid-Atlantic Ridge.

🌑 Iceland – land of fire and ice

Geologically, Iceland is one of the youngest countries in the world. Nowhere in Iceland is more than 20 million years old. It is situated right on the Mid-Atlantic Ridge, where the Eurasian and North American plates are tearing apart. This means that volcanic eruptions are a constant threat. Since the island was first inhabited in the ninth century, there have been more than 150 recorded volcanic eruptions. These eruptions also create new land, such as the Westman Islands, off the south coast of the mainland.

The rift between the two plates is visible at several locations in Iceland. At Thingvellir in the south-west of the country, scientists have watched and measured the continents of Europe and America separating at a rate of 5 mm per year. In the last century, the trench has grown by approximately 50 cm. This is the narrowest gap between the two plates anywhere along the ridge.

As well as the shape of South America and Africa, Wegener used evidence from the rocks in these regions to support his theory. The mountains running across South Africa seemed to link to those in Argentina in South America. Also, in his studies of layers of rock sequences, Wegener discovered that the lower layers – and therefore the oldest – were the same on both sides of the Atlantic Ocean, which divides the two land masses. Wegener suggested that these ancient layers were made when the continents were all part of a single land mass. Fossil plant species were also common across both regions. Many of these organisms could not possibly have travelled across the oceans that now separate the different continents.

Despite this evidence, Wegener's ideas were not generally accepted at the time. It was not until the 1960s that new evidence was found to support the theory of continental drift. By this time, scientists had a much better understanding of what happened on the ocean floors. It was clear that new ocean crust was continually being created. This in turn was helping to drive the movement of the continents. Wegener's original theory was put together with the newer ideas to form the overall theory we now know as plate tectonics.

◀◀ The huge crack in the ground pictured (left of centre) is part of the Mid-Atlantic Ridge, at Thingvellir in Iceland. This is one of the only places in the world where the ridge can be seen on the surface of the Earth. Almost everywhere else, mid-ocean ridges are deep below the water.

Oceanic and continental plates

Oceanic plates are the large slabs of oceanic or continental crust. They are composed of basalt, which is a heavy rock, so they tend to sink deeper into the Earth's mantle.
Continental plates are made of granite, which is much lighter than basalt, so these plates tend to rise and float above the oceanic plates. They are also much thinner than the oceanic plates.

▶▶ In 1963 a completely new island emerged from the sea to the south of the Icelandic mainland. It was named Surtsey, after Surtr, a fire giant from Norwegian mythology. The creation of islands like Surtsey is just one consequence of plate movement.

▼ Scientists believe that the movement of the Earth's plates is driven by convection currents in the mantle.

Why is the Earth's surface moving?

What is it that can cause plates the size of a continent to move? Many scientists believe that it is heat from within the Earth that powers the movement of the plates on its surface. At temperatures of over 1,000°C, the rocks in the mantle near the core become 'plastic' and start to flow towards the surface. It is only the high pressure of rocks in the crust from above that stops them from melting in the heat. Nearer the surface, the rocks cool, flow sideways and then return towards the core. It is believed that the rocks of the Earth's mantle form giant convection currents.

The sideways (lateral) movement of rocks just beneath the crust causes the plates on the surface to move. Where two currents move towards each other, the plates riding on them do the same; where two currents separate, so do the plates. This important difference results in the various types of plate boundary. The plates move at different speeds and in different directions. Although most of them only move as little as 1 cm per year, over millions of years this movement has completely changed the pattern of land and sea on the Earth's surface. It is still changing now.

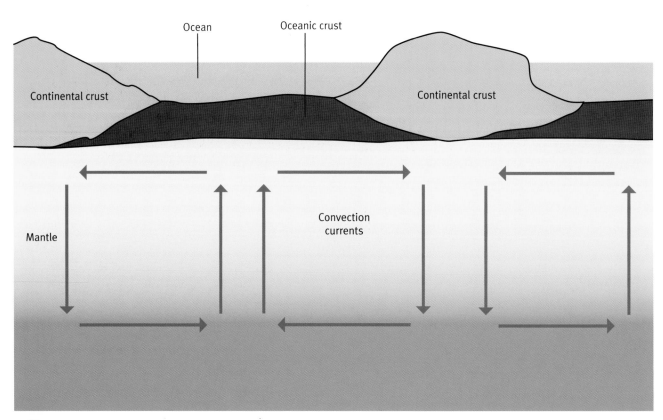

Continental Drift

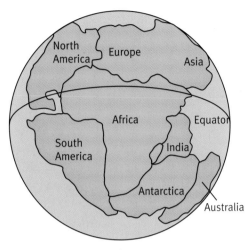

▲ The super-continent of Pangaea.

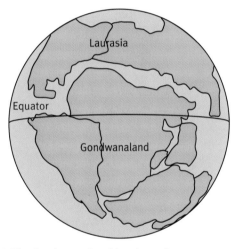

▲ The development and break-up of Laurasia and Gondwanaland.

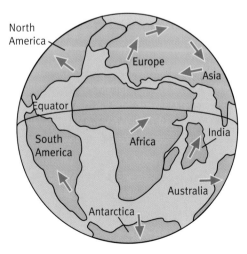

▲ The Earth 130 million years ago.

According to the theory of plate tectonics, all the continents were once joined together in a single massive land mass. This huge super-continent, called Pangaea, was surrounded by a giant ocean called Panthalassa. The diagrams on the left show the positions of present-day continents within Pangaea. Notice how little Africa has altered in all this time, but how far India has to travel before it becomes a part of Asia. Scientists believe that this land mass began to break up approximately 200 million years ago, as a result of the same processes that are at work today.

At first, Pangaea broke into two new continents called Laurasia and Gondwanaland. Europe, Asia and North America were all joined together as Laurasia. Gondwanaland was made up of Africa, Australia, South America and Antarctica. Until 150 million years ago, India still remained a part of this land mass.

After Laurasia and Gondwanaland broke apart, the continental land masses started to drift further. By 130 million years ago, the continents had begun to take the shapes that we are familiar with today. The Atlantic Ocean had started to form as Europe and North America drifted apart. Antarctica was moving south towards its current frozen climate – and India was on its way to crash into Asia.

🌑 A topsy-turvy world

Because of the movement of the continents, countries and places we know today were once in very different positions across the globe. The equator would once have cut through North America and, at one time in the far distant past, the Sahara Desert in Africa was positioned at the South Pole!

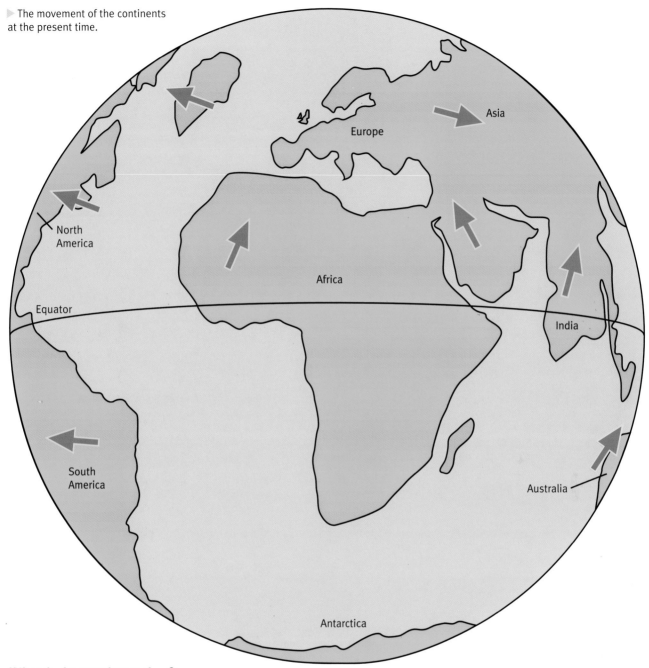

The movement of the continents at the present time.

What is happening today?

The arrows on the map show the directions in which the continents are currently moving. Europe and North America continue to drift further apart, making the Atlantic Ocean larger. Britain and the United States are moving further away from each other at a rate of around 2 cm a year! North and South America have joined, and Australia is moving northwards. India has at last completed its journey north and ploughed into Asia, creating the world's highest range of mountains, the Himalayas.

▶ The fossil of this long-extinct fish was found in the cliffs above Chaleur Bay in the Gaspe Peninsula in Canada. When it was alive it would have been swimming in seas close to the equator. However, the movement of the Earth's plates over millions of years has resulted in this bay being relocated to an extreme northern latitude.

🌑 The travelling continents

The continents have moved huge distances over the many millions of years of Earth's history. Sometime in the far-distant future, America may have drifted so far to the west that it will collide with Asia, and the Pacific Ocean will disappear altogether.

If the drift of the continents continues at its current rate, how will the world look in the future? The map below shows what the Earth's surface could look like 50 million years from now. Australia will be much further north than at present. North and South America will be separated, and Africa, turning clockwise, will have collided with Europe. However, we can only guess at what will happen this far in the future – nothing is certain. The surface of the Earth is in constant motion, shaping landforms and affecting people throughout the world. Even after all the land masses have collided and converged again in that far-distant future, they will start to break up once again, and will continue to do so for ever on this imperceptibly slow-moving but inevitable cycle.

▶ The world 50 million years from now.

▶▶ The high, jagged peaks of the Himalayan mountain range were caused by the collision of the plates carrying India and Asia millions of years ago. The Indian plate was made of solid rock, whereas the Asian plate was formed from softer sedimentary rock. As the plates collided, the softer rock on the edge of the Asian plate was forced upwards, creating mountains. Continuing plate movement in this region means that the Himalayas are still growing.

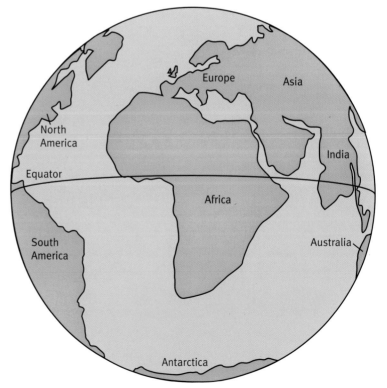

Plate Margins

The Earth's plates may move very slowly in human terms, but this movement is responsible for some of the most spectacular landscapes – and some of the most dangerous hazards – on our planet. These processes take place at the edges, or boundaries, of these plates, where two or more of them meet. The movement of convection currents in the Earth causes three different types of plate boundary depending on the movement of the plates:

▲ This black smoke is coming from an underwater vent in the Mid-Atlantic Ridge, where volcanic liquid is bubbling up through the Earth's crust.

- **Divergent** (constructive) boundary. This is where plates move apart.
- **Convergent** (destructive) boundary. This is where plates collide.
- **Transform** (conservative) boundary. This is where plates slide horizontally past one another.

At each of these boundaries, or plate margins, the type of movement causes different phenomena, and can even change the face of the Earth itself. Even though some plates seem to be moving independently of others, they are all connected: the movement of one plate can affect another one, even if it is thousands of kilometres away.

Divergent boundaries and mid-ocean ridges

Divergent boundaries occur where two plates move away from each other. They are pushed apart by molten rock, or magma, rising from the mantle beneath the crust. As soon as the magma reaches the surface it solidifies, forming new crust. This is why this type of plate boundary is sometimes called a constructive boundary.

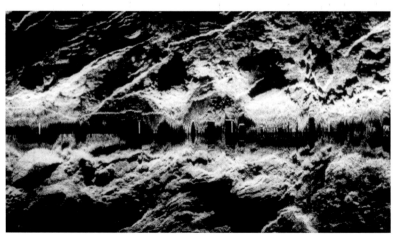

▶ This sonograph image shows the Reykjanes Ridge, part of the Mid-Atlantic Ridge that lies south of Iceland. The lighter areas are lava that has hardened and formed hills and hummocks (seen most clearly at lower left).

One of the most significant effects of plates moving apart in this way is the formation of mid-ocean ridges. As their name suggests, mid-ocean ridges run along the bottom of the world's oceans, at the boundaries of two plates pulling apart. They are essentially long chains of underwater mountains, stretching around 65,000 km through the Earth's oceans. Some of the mountains in the mid-ocean ridges are more than 3,500 metres high. The ridges are caused by the magma solidifying to fill the cracks caused by the divergent plates separating. The magma cools and attaches to the edge of the plates, where it quite literally renews the 'floor' of the Earth. This process is called sea-floor spreading. All plates have a 'leading edge' – the front of the plate as it is moving away – and a 'trailing edge' – the part at the back. The new crust is formed at the trailing edge, so the closer to the leading edge the crust is, the older it is. Mid-ocean ridges are where much of the immense heat from inside the Earth is released.

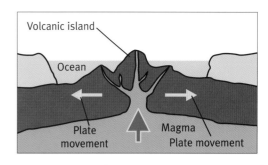

▲ A divergent plate boundary is where two plates are moving away from each other. Volcanic islands can be formed at divergent boundaries as magma forces its way up through the cracks between the plates.

▼ Mid-ocean ridges stretch across the sea floors around the world, formed by plates pulling away from each other. The locations of the ridges are shown in the map below.

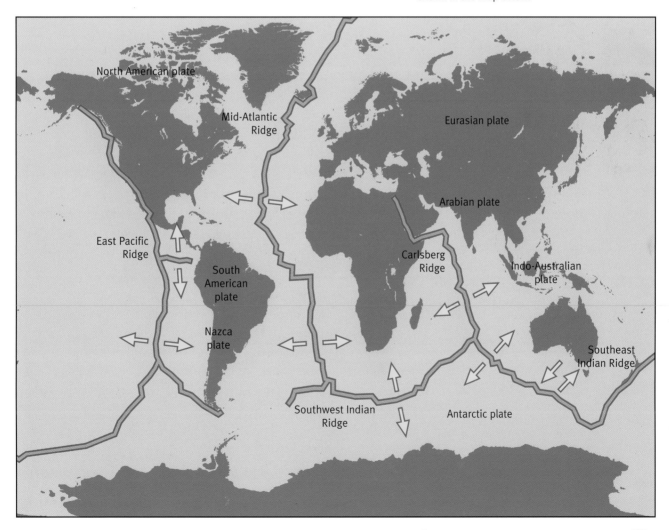

The Mid-Atlantic Ridge

Perhaps the best known mid-ocean ridge is the Mid-Atlantic Ridge. This extends right from the Arctic Ocean to beyond South Africa. Over the last 200 million years, the North American and Eurasian plates have been pushing apart at the Mid-Atlantic Ridge; this has created the Atlantic Ocean, which is still growing at just over 2 cm every year. Most of the Mid-Atlantic Ridge is below sea level, with the exception of the island of Iceland.

▷ Congealed lava on the Mid-Atlantic Ridge. The lava has been pushed up from the Earth's mantle, and then cooled and hardened by the ocean.

Where oceanic and continental plates collide

Convergent boundaries occur where two or more plates collide. The type of collision depends on the nature of the plates involved.

The Nazca plate to the west of South America is an oceanic plate (see page 10). It is colliding with the South American plate, which is a continental plate. As it does so, the Nazca plate is forced down underneath the South American plate. The area where this happens is called a subduction zone, and because the Earth's crust can be destroyed here, this type of boundary is sometimes called a destructive plate boundary. As the plates meet, a deep trench forms at the bottom of the sea. These ocean trenches form the deepest parts of the oceans. The Peru-Chile trench runs for thousands of kilometres along the eastern Pacific Ocean where the Nazca and South American plates meet. It ranges from 8 km to 10 km in depth. As the oceanic plate subducts, some of the sediment from the ocean floor is scraped off and joined to the leading edge of the continental plate on top. Scientists think this may be why the Andes mountains still seem to be growing – as the Nazca plate dives into the Peru-Chile trench, sediment is building beneath the mountains, forcing them upwards.

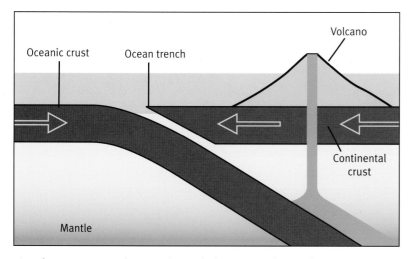

At destructive boundaries, where oceanic and continental plates meet, the oceanic plate can be forced down beneath the continental plate, forming a subduction zone. Ocean trenches, earthquakes and volcanoes are all features of destructive boundaries.

As the oceanic plate is forced downwards, violent collisions take place between the two plates. These are earthquakes. When the crust carries on descending, it melts due to friction and the higher temperatures that exist in the Earth's mantle. The melting crust forms magma. Some of this newly formed magma rises to the surface in the form of volcanoes.

▼ The Andes mountains were formed by the subduction of the Nazca plate under the South American plate. Scientists believe that the Andes are getting higher as the plate movement continues in this way.

Trench-flipping

The collision of an oceanic and a continental plate can also cause a phenomenon called trench-flipping. The continental material cannot sink so it moves into a trench, where it gets stuck. Its leading edge becomes squashed or folded into mountains. This in turn causes some of the oceanic crust to sit on top of the continental material. Pressure in this region grows until it forces the trench to 'flip' – the oceanic plate moves back under the continental crust.

Eventually two continents will crash into each other. When this happens, the trench disappears and new mountain ranges can be formed. It is possible for a plate to disappear altogether, but this would only occur if a plate was diving into a subduction trench more quickly than the new crust was being formed at the trailing edge. This could have dramatic consequences, though, as the disappearance of a whole plate would cause changes in the positioning of all the others on Earth.

▼ This sonar image shows an area of subduction on the floor of the Pacific Ocean off the coast of North America, where the Juan de Fuca plate is being pushed down by the North American plate. This causes sediments to build up into the ridges seen along the middle of the image. The colours represent the depth of the ocean: orange is 1,000 metres, yellow is 2,000 metres and green is 3,000 metres.

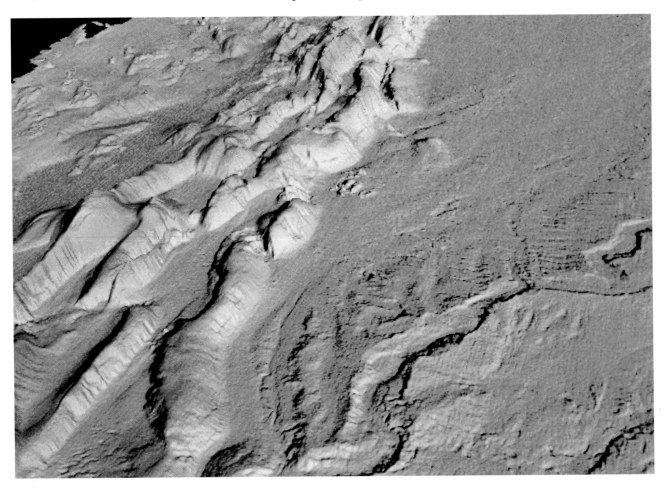

Challenger Deep

The Pacific and Philippine plates are two colliding oceanic plates. The Marianas Trench marks the location where the two plates meet. Challenger Deep is at the southern end of the Marianas Trench. It is the lowest part of any ocean, reaching nearly 11 km below sea level.

▷ Challenger Deep is the lowest part of any ocean on Earth.

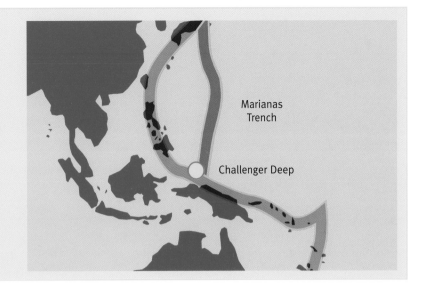

Marianas Trench

Challenger Deep

Where ocean plates collide

Where two oceanic plates meet, one is usually pushed underneath the other, and the processes involved are the same as when oceanic and continental plates meet. As the plates collide, the younger of them will move over the older plate because it is less dense. The older plate bends under the pressure and is forced deeper into the Earth, forming a huge trench. As the plate descends, it can trigger earthquakes that can affect continents, even though they are caused by oceanic plates.

◁ A computer model showing the region surrounding the Marianas Trench in the Pacific Ocean. The depth of the ocean is colour coded: dark green areas are land, pink areas are nearest to the surface, through yellow, green and blue. The deepest point – the trench itself – is coloured purple.

▲ This is a satellite image of the Aleutian islands in Alaska, forming an island arc. They lie at the northern edge of the Pacific Ring of Fire.

The descending plate heats up and, at great depths, the rock begins to melt, forming magma. The magma begins the return journey, rising towards the surface. It bubbles up at the leading edge, cools down, and joins on to the crust, forming volcanoes. These grow bigger as the process continues, until they are so high that they rise above the surface of the water, forming a string of volcanic islands called an island arc. The islands of the Caribbean and the Aleutian islands were formed in this way.

🌑 The Pacific Ring of Fire

The Ring of Fire is the name given to the most famous island arc – the huge chain of volcanoes surrounding the Pacific Ocean. It gets its name from the frequency of active volcanoes, and from the large number of volcanoes that have not recently erupted (dormant volcanoes). Three-quarters of the world's volcanoes can be found here. The Ring of Fire extends from South to North America, to Japan, then right down to New Zealand.

▶ The ocean trenches surrounding the Pacific Ring of Fire.

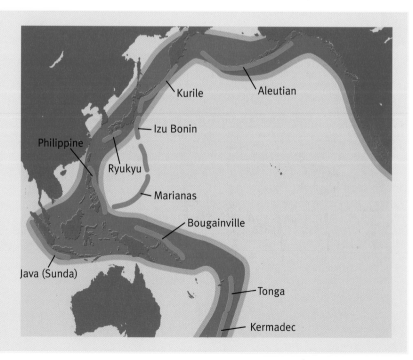

🌐 The Himalayan mountains

The Indo-Australian plate collided with the Eurasian plate 50 million years ago. It is still moving north at a rate of 5 cm per year. The boundary between the two plates was buckled and forced upwards, forming the Himalayan mountains – the highest mountain range on Earth. As the plates continue to collide, the world's highest mountains are getting higher.

▶ Mount Everest in the Himalayas is the highest mountain in the world. As the two plates collide, it is still gaining height.

Where continental plates collide

Scientists once believed that mountains were formed millions of years ago when the Earth was very young. They thought that the planet had once been a molten ball and that as it cooled down, its surface cracked and folded up on itself, throwing up the peaks of the world's mountain ranges. Later, as their understanding of the Earth grew, scientists realised that this theory did not quite work; it would mean that all the mountain ranges would be roughly the same age – very old indeed – and they knew this was not the case. Today, we know that mountains are a result of the collision between two continental plates.

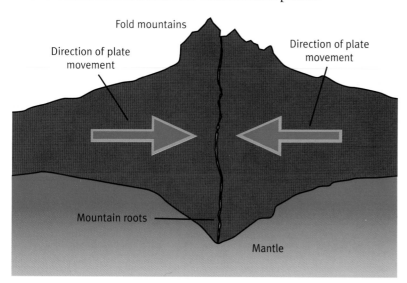

Fold mountains

Direction of plate movement

Direction of plate movement

Mountain roots

Mantle

◀ The collision of two continental plates forces huge amounts of rock upwards. After many thousands of years these build into mountain ranges like the Himalayas; they are called fold mountains because the Earth 'folded' upwards to form them.

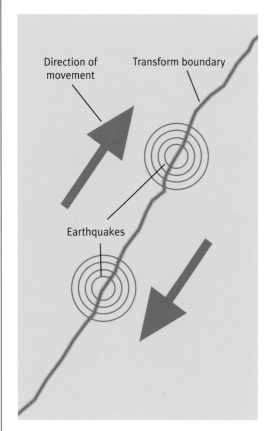

Direction of movement

Transform boundary

Earthquakes

▲ Earthquakes occur at transform plate boundaries, where two plates are grinding against each other.

When two continental plates meet, neither plate is pushed downwards (subducted). Instead, they collide and are buckled upwards. It is this action that creates fold mountains. When the two plates meet, enormous piles of crumpled rock are forced upwards to build up on the Earth's surface. Over many years, the rocks are weathered to form the jagged peaks we associate with mountains today. The Himalayas and the Andes mountain ranges were formed in this way. Although they appear to be very old, in fact these mountains were only formed in the last 50 million years, and are therefore relatively young in terms of the Earth's long history.

Transform boundaries and faults

Not all the Earth's plates are moving apart or crashing into one another. Some plates slide horizontally against each other, at transform boundaries. No crust is created or destroyed at these boundaries, which is why they are sometimes called 'conservative' plate boundaries. This means that there are no volcanoes. However, the movement of these giant plates releases enormous amounts of energy, as the plates tend to stick then slip violently rather than sliding smoothly against each other. The movement at transform boundaries can cause fractures in the Earth's crust, called faults. Fold mountains and earthquakes are common features of faults.

▷ A seismologist (a scientist who studies earthquakes) investigates an area of earthquake activity. The cracks in the Earth are still steaming.

▷▷ Emergency services at work after the earthquake in San Francisco in October 1989. The city lies on the San Andreas Fault and is subject to many earthquakes caused by plate movement.

🌐 The San Andreas Fault

The San Andreas Fault marks the boundary between the Pacific and North American plates. Both plates are moving in a north-westerly direction, but the Pacific plate is moving more quickly (6 cm per year, compared with 1 cm for the North American plate). The San Andreas Fault is over 1,300 km long. The plates do not slide easily against each other, and earthquakes occur when there is sudden movement. As this part of the United States is heavily populated, these earthquakes can cause severe disruption and loss of life. A major earthquake could happen at any time along the San Andreas Fault. If the present movement of the plates continues for many years, Los Angeles will eventually be north of San Francisco!

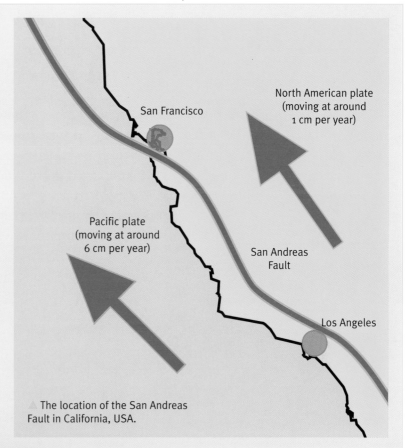

△ The location of the San Andreas Fault in California, USA.

▲ Lava erupts from the Stromboli volcano in Italy. Activity in this region occurs at a plate boundary zone, where the exact location of the meeting plates is unknown.

Plate boundary zones

Not every plate boundary fits easily into one of these categories. Some are so complicated that it is difficult to know the exact location of the boundary. Scientists have worked out where they think the plate boundaries are through charting the incidences of phenomena such as earthquakes and volcanoes, and have worked out where most activity takes place. The effects of plate movements may also extend over a large area, not just where the two plates meet. In these situations there is a plate boundary zone. An example of such a zone is the Mediterranean region of Europe, where the African and Eurasian plates meet. The volcanoes and earthquakes of Italy are caused by the meeting of the two plates in this zone.

Rifts and hot spots

Activity related to the Earth's tectonic plates can even happen away from the boundaries. Sometimes a plate carrying a continent can actually split apart. This happens

🌎 The Great Rift Valley

The Great Rift Valley is the most famous example of a rift in the Earth caused by tectonic movement. It stretches for 3,000 km down East Africa. The valley ranges from nearly 400 metres below sea level to nearly 2,000 metres above sea level, and has many lakes, rivers, and high jagged cliffs along its course. Because of the way it was formed – through the weakening of the Earth's crust by magma beneath its surface – the area of the Great Rift Valley is volcanically active. Mount Kilimanjaro – the highest point in Africa – is probably the best-known volcanic mountain in the region, although it is believed to be extinct.

▶ The Great Rift Valley running through central Kenya in Africa.

Mountains on Mars

As technology allows us to see the other planets in our Solar System in increasing detail, scientists have begun to wonder whether plate activity might be at work elsewhere in the Universe. There are many features on the planet Mars, for example, that are similar to those on the surface of the Earth. Among these are craters, rifts and volcanoes. Volcanic eruptions have also been seen on Jupiter's moons, and the landscape of the planet Venus is characterised by lava plains.

▼ Olympus Mons is the largest known volcano in the Solar System. Situated on the planet Mars, it rises 27 km above the surrounding land (for comparison, Mount Everest is only 8.8 km high!). Has plate movement beneath the surface of the planet caused this?

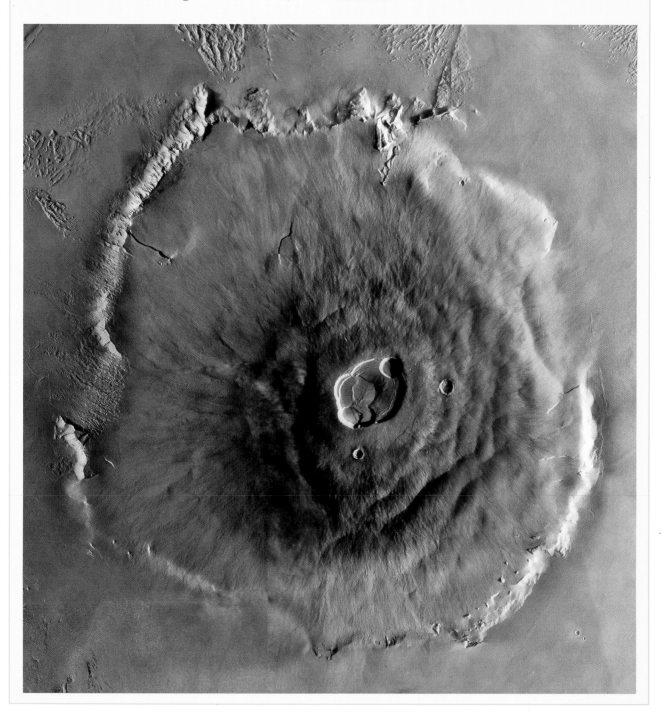

> ▶▶ Fountains of lava spewing from Mauna Loa – one of five active volcanoes on the main Hawaiian island.

> ▶ Lava can flow at speeds of up to 50 kph from volcanoes like Kilauea, on the Pacific hot spot.

> ▼ The Hawaiian islands, as seen from space. This chain of islands in the Pacific Ocean is formed by a series of volcanoes moving over a hot spot in the Earth's crust.

when magma builds up towards continental crust, making it weaker and eventually causing it to crack. Parts of the crust drop, forming an immense rift valley. These valleys are actually ocean basins – the first stage in the formation of a new ocean and, eventually, a new tectonic plate. Over a long period of time, the sea will fill the rift. As this happens the rift – now under the water – will develop a lava ridge of mountains. All the mid-ocean ridges began in this way, by the creation of a series of rift valleys.

Although most of the Earth's volcanoes lie at the edge of tectonic plates, there are some that are situated a long way from these boundaries. These are called intra-plate volcanoes. Most of these volcanoes are dormant, but several are still active – the most famous of these are Mauna Loa and Kilauea on the Hawaiian islands in the Pacific Ocean. They exist because they are situated over hot spots. A hot spot is a huge fountain of lava beneath the surface of the Earth, which burns through the crust where it is thinner than normal, to form a volcano. The lava fountain always stays in the same place, but as the plate moves above it, the existing volcanoes are moved away from the hot spot and new volcanoes are formed. In Hawaii there is a string of dead volcanoes like this – each one was formed by sitting over the hot spot and has now been moved on by plate movement. The active volcanoes are the ones currently over the hot spot.

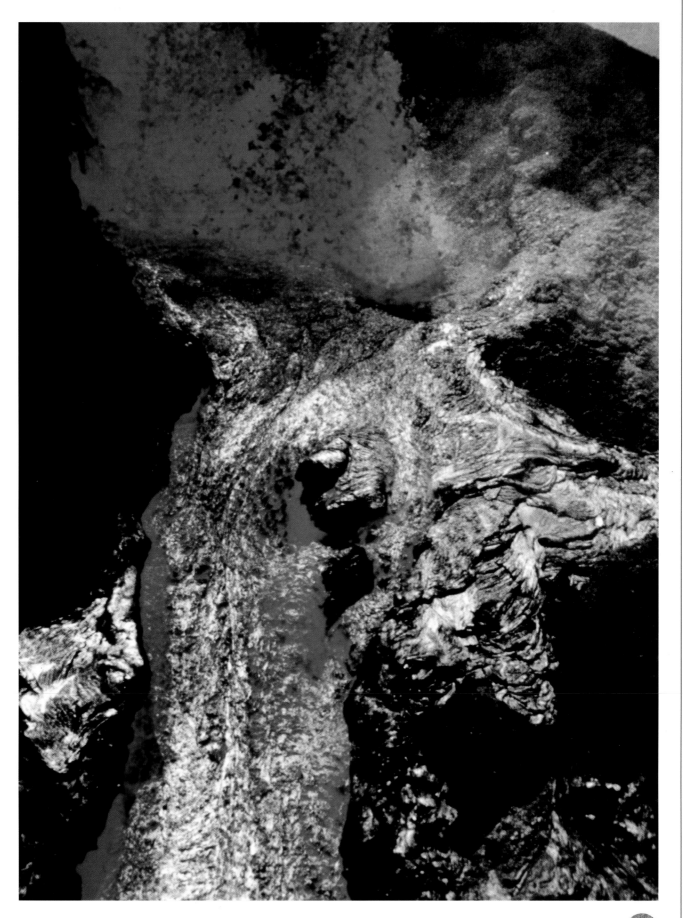

The Hazards Caused by Plate Movements

Although the movements of plates and continents are imperceptible to us, over many years these processes have created some of the most spectacular scenery in the world. However, these same movements can also cause some serious hazards. Two of the most destructive of these are earthquakes and volcanic eruptions.

The understanding we now have of plate tectonics helps to explain the location of earthquakes and volcanoes. Earthquakes occur only in narrow belts across the Earth and there are similar zones of activity for volcanoes. It is at the plate boundaries, where they are moving together or spreading apart, that earthquakes and volcanic eruptions take place.

▼ The concentration of earthquake activity around the world. It is clear from the map that earthquakes occur in 'belts' around the plate margins.

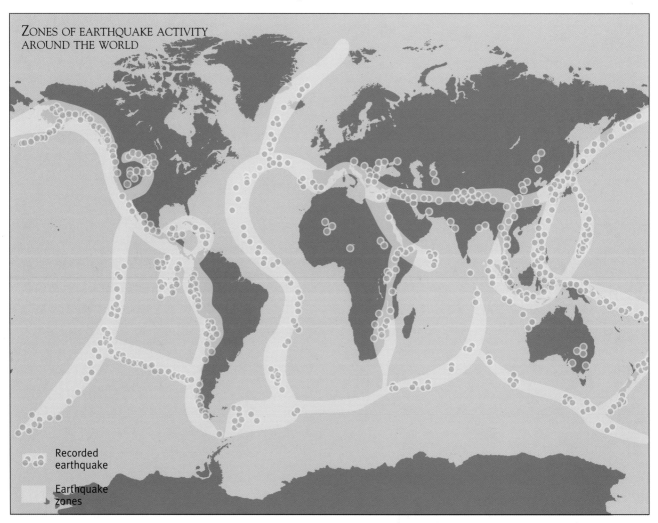

ZONES OF EARTHQUAKE ACTIVITY
AROUND THE WORLD

Recorded earthquake

Earthquake zones

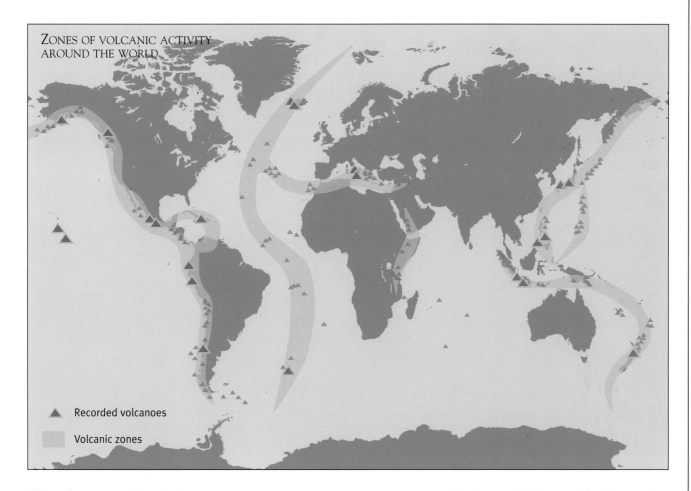

ZONES OF VOLCANIC ACTIVITY AROUND THE WORLD

▲ Recorded volcanoes

▢ Volcanic zones

What is an earthquake?

An earthquake is a sudden release of energy in the Earth's crust or upper part of the mantle. Earthquakes usually occur when two plates moving in different directions become stuck, at a time when the pressure is suddenly released.

The actual location of an earthquake is often underground. This location is called the focus. The place on the Earth's surface directly above this is called the epicentre. If the focus is near to the surface, an earthquake is likely to cause more damage than if it is located far underground.

▲ Volcanic zones also lie around the plate margins, although they are concentrated in fewer regions than earthquake activity. The Hawaiian islands in the Pacific Ocean are formed from volcanoes such as Mauna Loa and Kilauea.

▼ An earthquake is caused when parts of two plates sliding past each other get locked. Enormous tension builds up and eventually rock gives way. The tension is released in the form of energy, or seismic waves that send out vibrations in all directions.

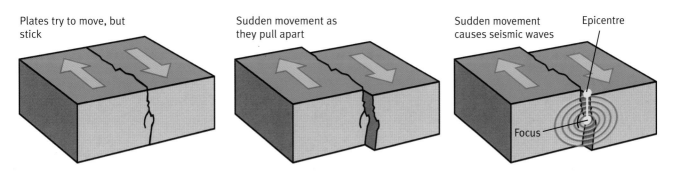

Plates try to move, but stick

Sudden movement as they pull apart

Sudden movement causes seismic waves

Epicentre

Focus

🌑 Tsunamis

Tsunamis are huge waves of water caused by the sudden vertical movement of the sea floor during an earthquake. They can also be caused by volcanic eruptions or landslides beneath the sea. In the deep ocean, the height of a tsunami is usually no more than 1 metre, but the waves can travel at over 650 kph. As tsunamis reach shallow water they slow down and the height of the waves increases dramatically, sometimes reaching 25 metres when approaching land. The earthquake responsible for the series of tsunamis across Asia in December 2004 was caused when the Indian plate slipped beneath the Eurasian plate. The sea floor was thrust upwards, creating massive amounts of energy that sent giant waves racing across the Indian Ocean. Because tsunamis travel and build so quickly, there was little warning – and the devastation was widespread.

▲ A man searches among the wreckage on a beach in Phuket, Thailand, after a tsunami struck in December 2004. The massive wave was caused by an undersea earthquake.

When an earthquake occurs, the tension or energy is released as a series of seismic waves. It is these waves that cause the destruction usually associated with earthquakes. The first waves to arrive are called 'P' waves. These travel upwards through the Earth's crust at nearly 25,000 kph. It is the slower 'S' waves that generally cause more damage. The movement in these waves is horizontal rather than vertical: they shake the ground sideways. Buildings and roads are more easily damaged by horizontal than by vertical movement.

The effects of earthquakes

Some of the effects of an earthquake happen straight away; these are primary effects. Others cause problems over a longer period of time, and are called secondary effects. The collapse of buildings is a primary effect because it happens immediately. A secondary effect is that many people will be made homeless, and it will take a long time to re-house them all.

The amount of damage caused by an earthquake, and the number of people killed or injured, will vary from one earthquake to another. This is due to a number of factors:

The location of the focus: If this is near the surface, the earthquake is likely to cause more damage.
The location of the earthquake: If it hits a city, it is likely that more damage will be caused, and more people killed, than an earthquake in the countryside.
The country in which an earthquake takes place: The effects of earthquakes are usually much greater in poor countries. Buildings are generally less able to cope with an earthquake, and poor countries often have to wait for international aid.
The time of day: If an earthquake happens at night, most people will be asleep. They will not be able to get out of buildings in time, and so more people will be killed or injured.
The number of smaller earthquakes that follow the main one as the ground settles: These are called aftershocks, and can cause great damage to already weakened buildings.

One serious effect of earthquakes is damage to homes and transport – roads can be cracked open and flyovers can collapse. This damaged flyover is in California.

The earthquake that destroyed Bam

The city of Bam in south-east Iran lies near the boundary between the Iranian and Indian plates. The region is frequently hit by earthquakes. On the morning of 26 December 2003, an earthquake measuring 6.6 on the Richter scale devastated the city, destroying 80 per cent of the buildings, including a fortress that had stood for over 2,000 years. Some slight earth tremors had been felt the previous day, but this is not unusual for the region, so people took little notice. The first earthquake was still only minor and did not cause much damage. However, in the early hours of the morning, the second and stronger earthquake struck. Its epicentre was the southern edge of the city of Bam. Over 26,000 of the city's 120,000 population were killed in the earthquake. It is estimated that the long-term cost of repairing the damage caused by the Bam earthquake will be nearly £1 billion.

▶ The city of Bam in Iran was reduced to rubble by an earthquake in December 2003.

Earthquakes in the British Isles

The British Isles do not lie on the boundary between two plates, and so do not experience major earthquakes. It is not true, however, to say that there are never earthquakes in the British Isles. Any movement in the Earth's crust, even if it is slight, can cause an earthquake. Notice that, unlike earthquakes concentrated on plate boundaries, those in the British Isles are widely scattered. The map shows the location of the earthquakes recorded in the twentieth century. The biggest of these happened in 1931, at Dogger Bank in the North Sea. This earthquake measured 6.1 on the Richter scale.

▶ The location and magnitude of earthquakes that hit the British Isles in the twentieth century.

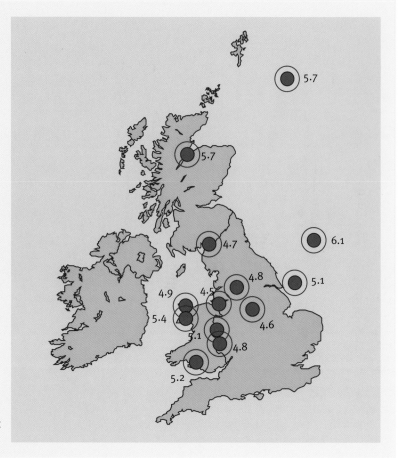

▲ Mount Vesuvius was responsible for burying the city of Pompeii in Italy in AD 79. Vesuvius is dormant, but may erupt again one day.

▶▶ Mount Etna is the most active volcano in Europe. Here, a great column of ash rises above the mountain during the most explosive volcanic eruption of the last century.

Volcanic eruptions

A volcano is formed when magma from the mantle rises up through cracks in the Earth's crust and erupts on to the surface. Above the surface the magma solidifies and is called lava. Like earthquakes, most volcanic eruptions take place at or near the boundaries of plates. They are natural events and only become hazards to people when they erupt near areas of human settlement.

Many of the world's volcanoes have erupted recently, and may do so again in the near future. These are called active volcanoes. Mount Etna in Italy is the most active volcano in Europe. Some volcanoes have not erupted for hundreds of years, but may still erupt again in the future. These volcanoes, like Vesuvius in Italy, are called dormant volcanoes. The third type of volcanoes are extinct volcanoes. These will never erupt again. The area of Le Puy in France is characterised by extinct volcanoes, which are being gradually worn away.

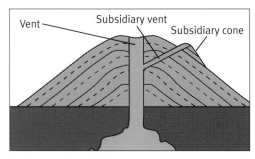

Vent Subsidiary vent Subsidiary cone

▲ A composite volcano.

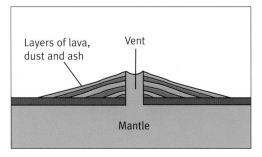

Layers of lava, dust and ash Vent

Mantle

▲ A shield volcano.

Types of volcano

Not all volcanoes are exactly the same. Their size and shape depend mainly on the type of magma in an eruption. The most common types of volcano are composite, shield and caldera volcanoes.

Some of the world's most spectacular and beautiful mountains are composite volcanoes. Magma rises to the surface of the Earth through a central vent, and the volcano may also have secondary or smaller vents. The volcano grows in size as eruptions pour more lava on to the surface, along with dust and ash. Composite volcanoes are usually very steep sided, such as Mount Fuji in Japan.

Shield volcanoes are built up from huge and repeated lava flows. The lava erupts slowly and spreads over a wide area.

⊕ The Soufriere Hills volcano, Montserrat

Montserrat is an island in the Caribbean Sea. It is part of the island arc formed where the Caribbean plate is colliding with the North American and South American plates. After hundreds of years as a dormant volcano, the composite Soufriere Hills volcano on Montserrat erupted in 1997. Eruptions of the volcano continued for several months, until 26 December, when the top of the volcano collapsed. A cloud of ash and dust was thrown 5,000 metres in to the atmosphere. Nineteen people were killed in the main eruptions, and the whole island was covered in a thick layer of ash. The volcano continues to show signs of activity but these are at a low level, and are carefully monitored.

▶ Thick clouds of steam and ash billowing from the Soufriere Hills volcano.

Some of the largest volcanoes in the world are shield volcanoes. The Hawaiian islands are made of a series of shield volcanoes. The largest of these, Mauna Loa, reaches over 4,000 metres above sea level. Mauna Loa is really over 9,000 metres in height – another 5,000 metres of the volcano is hidden below sea level. Surtsey, in Iceland, is another example of a shield volcano.

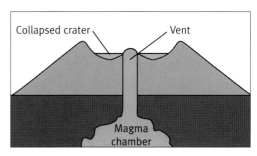
▲ A caldera volcano.

The largest and most violent volcanic eruptions come from caldera volcanoes. They hurl hundreds of cubic kilometres of magma on to the surface of the Earth. When so much magma is suddenly removed from under a volcano, the ground collapses and the whole summit of the volcano is blown away, to form a huge hollow called a caldera. Some calderas are several kilometres in width and depth, and often contain lakes, or have been flooded by the sea. Krakatoa in Indonesia is an example of a caldera volcano.

🌑 Volcano damage

Lava flows destroy anything in their paths. Scientists have tried various methods of stopping or redirecting them but with little success. The most violent eruptions explode fragments of rock out of a volcano. These rocks travel down the sides of a volcano at speeds of over 150 kph. Most of the 30,000 people killed when Mount Pelée in Martinique erupted in 1902 were killed by these pyroclastic flows. Clouds of dust and ash fall after explosive eruptions. This dust can ruin crops, damage transport and communications, and be harmful to people's health. The dust and ash may rise high in to the atmosphere and cut out some of the Sun's rays.

▶ When Mount Pinatubo in the Philippines erupted in 1991, it hurled 20 million tonnes of material in to the atmosphere. This circled the globe, and reduced temperatures around the world by 0.5°C.

Glossary

active volcano A volcano that erupts regularly and may do so at any time.

aftershocks Earthquake waves that occur after the main earthquake.

caldera A large volcanic crater formed by the collapse of the cone of a volcano during a very explosive eruption.

composite volcano A volcano made of alternate layers of ash and lava; it may have side (subsidiary) vents and cones.

continental crust Parts of the Earth's crust made of light rocks. They are made of compounds containing lots of silica (sand) and aluminium.

continental drift The theory by Alfred Wegener to explain why the Earth's continents appear to move and split into different sections.

convection current A current of hot magma in the mantle. It rises from the lower part of the mantle, where temperatures are hottest, towards the crust.

convergent boundary A boundary at which two plates are moving towards each other. The denser plate dips down below the other and melts.

core The central section of the Earth; the inner core is solid, and the outer core is molten.

crust The surface or outer layer of the Earth.

crystalline rocks Rocks containing crystals, for example quartz and feldspar.

divergent boundary Where two or more plates are moving apart, often resulting in mid-ocean ridges and volcanic islands; also called a constructive boundary.

dormant volcano A volcano that has not recently erupted, but may do so again.

earthquake A sudden and often violent movement caused by release of pressure in rocks deep below the Earth's surface.

epicentre The point on the Earth's surface vertically above the focus, where the worst damage usually occurs in an earthquake.

extinct volcano A volcano that no longer erupts.

fault A fracture in the Earth's crust caused by the movement of plates at transform boundaries; earthquakes are frequent occurrences along faults.

focus The point underground from which an earthquake originates.

fold mountains Mountains made of a set of parallel ridges caused when the continental rocks 'pile up' at a destructive boundary or collision zone.

fossil The compacted and hardened remains of creatures that died millions of years ago.

geothermal energy Energy derived from natural underground heat in rocks.

Gondwanaland A continent formed after the split of the original super-continent of Pangaea, comprising Africa, Australia, South America and Antarctica.

hot spot An area on the Earth's surface where the crust is quite thin. Magma can break through and form a volcano.

inner core The solid inner part of the central section of the Earth.

intra-plate A point within a plate not near its edges.

island arc A chain of islands formed when volcanoes created on the ocean floor grow tall enough to break the surface.

Laurasia A continent formed after the split of the original super-continent of Pangaea, comprising Europe, Asia and North America.

lava Magma that erupts on to the surface of the Earth through a vent or fissure in a volcano.

leading edge The edge of a plate that is furthest away for the adjoining plate; the leading edge is made up of the oldest rock.

lithosphere The solid outer layer of the Earth, from the Greek *lithos*, meaning 'stone'.

magma Molten rock present beneath the Earth's surface.

magnitude The amount of energy released in an earthquake.

mantle The layer of the Earth above the core and beneath the crust.

Mid-Atlantic Ridge The name given to the mid-ocean ridge stretching down the centre of the Atlantic Ocean.

mid-ocean ridges Zones on the ocean floor where oceanic plates are moving apart and new crust is being created.

natural hazard Something likely to result in loss of life or damage to property that is not caused by people.

oceanic crust The thinnest and youngest parts of the Earth's crust, largely made up of the dense rock basalt.

ocean trenches Deep oceanic areas where one plate is dragged beneath another.

outer core The molten outer part of the central section of the Earth.

P waves Primary or 'push' waves; earthquake waves that travel from the epicentre up to the surface of the Earth.

Pangaea The Earth's original super-continent, in which all the present continents formed one huge land mass.

Panthalassa The Earth's original single ocean surrounding the super-continent of Pangaea.

plate-boundary zone A broad region where two or more plates meet but where the exact boundaries are not certain.

plate tectonics The theory developed in the 1960s from earlier ideas of continental drift. It explains the nature of the Earth's plates, the way they move and the features that form at their boundaries, including earthquakes and volcanoes.

plates The moving slabs of rock that make up the Earth's crust. There are nine large plates and several smaller ones.

primary effects The immediate effect of an earthquake.

pyroclastic flow Volcanic ash, dust, bombs and other fragments in hot, dense gases, which roll downhill at high speed.

Richter scale A scale for measuring the energy or magnitude of an earthquake.

rift A valley formed when a plate cracks in the middle of a continent.

S waves Secondary or 'shake' waves; earthquake waves that travel away from epicentre.

sea-floor spreading The renewal of the Earth's crust formed by magma bubbling up through the mantle, then cooling and hardening on contact with the ocean.

secondary effects The long-term effects of an earthquake.

sedimentary rock A type of rock formed from sediment that is compressed over time until it becomes solid.

seismic waves Movements in the Earth's crust that indicate that an earthquake may be about to happen or is already happening.

seismologist A scientist or geologist who studies earthquakes.

shield volcano A broad volcano built up by large and repeated lava flows.

subduction zone A destructive plate boundary where a dense oceanic plate is forced down below a lighter continental one, where it melts.

trailing edge The edge of a plate closest to the adjoining plate; new crust is being formed all the time at the trailing edge of plates and it is therefore made up of the youngest rock.

transform boundary Where two or more plates slide horizontally past each other; also known as a conservative boundary.

tremor A mild shaking on the surface of the Earth, usually an indication that an earthquake is about to occur.

trench-flipping The sudden reversal of subduction when an oceanic and continental plate meet.

tsunami A large wave caused by an undersea earthquake or volcanic eruption.

vent The hollow central part of a volcano, out of which lava, steam and other materials are ejected.

volcano A crack in the Earth's crust, through which molten rock, gases, ash and dust erupt.

volcanic eruption The emission of solid, liquid and gaseous material from a volcano.

weathering The wearing away of rock by rain, frost, plant roots and animals burrowing.

zone of activity An area within which earthquakes or volcanic eruptions are likely to take place.

Further Information

Books

Amazing Planet Earth by John Farndon et al: Southwater, 2001

Hazards and Responses by Victoria Bishop: HarperCollins Publishers, 2001

The Kingfisher Geography Encyclopedia by Clive Gifford: Kingfisher Publications, 2003

Volcanoes and Earthquakes by Rebecca Hunter: Discovering Geography, Raintree, 2003

Web sites

http://www.enchantedlearning.com/subjects/astronomy/planets/earth/Continents
A colourful site with maps and text explaining how tectonics works.

http://www.georesources.co.uk/
A large web site with several links to geography topics including earthquakes and volcanoes, organised by age and interest group.

http://www.platetectonics.com
A fascinating site with many articles and links giving information about how our planet is in constant change.

http://www.thirteen.org/savageearth/index
Learn about the Earth's major tectonic plates and the natural hazards caused by their movement such as earthquakes and volcanoes.

http://www.usgs.gov/
Home page of the US Geological Survey, with vast amounts of resources and news stories about the geography and geology of the United States, including information and updates about earthquakes and volcanoes.

Index

Acknowledgements

About the author

John Edwards has taught geography for more than 20 years, which he now combines with his work as a consultant and inspector for Warwickshire Education Authority, with responsibility for the provision of humanities subjects for the county's 240 primary and secondary schools. His published works include *Geography in Action*, *Environments* and a number of teachers' resource packs for OUP. He has also worked as series editor on the geography KeyFile series and contributor to the Geoactive series, as well as a number of web-based geography information projects.

About the consultant

Simon Ross is Head of Geography at Queen's College in Taunton, Somerset. He has published extensively on all aspects of physical geography, from introductory level to upper secondary. His books include *Natural Hazards*, *Introducing Physical Geography and Map Reading*, and several books in the series Geography 21. He has worked as editor on many series, including Longman Co-Ordinated Geography and Longman Exploring Geography. He has also acted as consultant on television programmes for the BBC, and for the QCA on Geography Key Stage 3 resources. He regularly lectures and contributes articles to encyclopedias and journals.

Picture Credits

Cover: **(t)** US Geological Survey/Science Photo Library **(bl)** © Pierre Vauthey/Corbis Sygma **(br)** Bernhard Edmaier/Science Photo Library **6** Bernhard Edmaier/Science Photo Library **7** Dr Ken MacDonald/Science Photo Library **11(t)** Planetary Visions Ltd/Science Photo Library **11(b)** Science Photo Library **12** Bernhard Edmaier/Science Photo Library **15** © Pierre Vauthey/Corbis Sygma **18(t)** © Jonathan Blair/Corbis **19** J. P. Danvoye, Publiphoto Diffusion/ Science Photo Library **20(t)** B. Murton/Southampton Oceanography Centre/Science Photo Library **20(b)** Institute of Oceanographic Sciences/NERC/Science Photo Library **22** © Ralph White/Corbis **23(b)** Will & Den McIntyre/Science Photo Library **24** W. Haxby, Lamont-Doherty Earth Observatory/Science Photo Library **25(b)** US Geological Survey/Science Photo Library **26(t)** NASA/Science Photo Library **27(t)** Simon Fraser/Science Photo Library **28(r)** © Roger Ressmeyer/ Corbis **29(b)** Peter Menzel/Science Photo Library **30(t)** © Roger Ressmeyer/Corbis **30(b)** © Wolfgang Kaehler/Corbis **31** US Geological Survey/Science Photo Library **32(t)** G. Brad Lewis/Science Photo Library **32(b)** NASA/Science Photo Library **33** Stephen & Donna O'Meara/Science Photo Library **36** © Luis Ascui/Reuters/Corbis **37(t)** Ed Young/Science Photo Library **37(b)** © Shahpari Sohale/Corbis **38(b)** Mauro Fermariello/Science Photo Library **39** Bernhard Edmaier/Science Photo Library **40(b)** Stephen & Donna O'Meara/Science Photo Library **41(b)** Robert M. Carey, NOAA/Science Photo Library